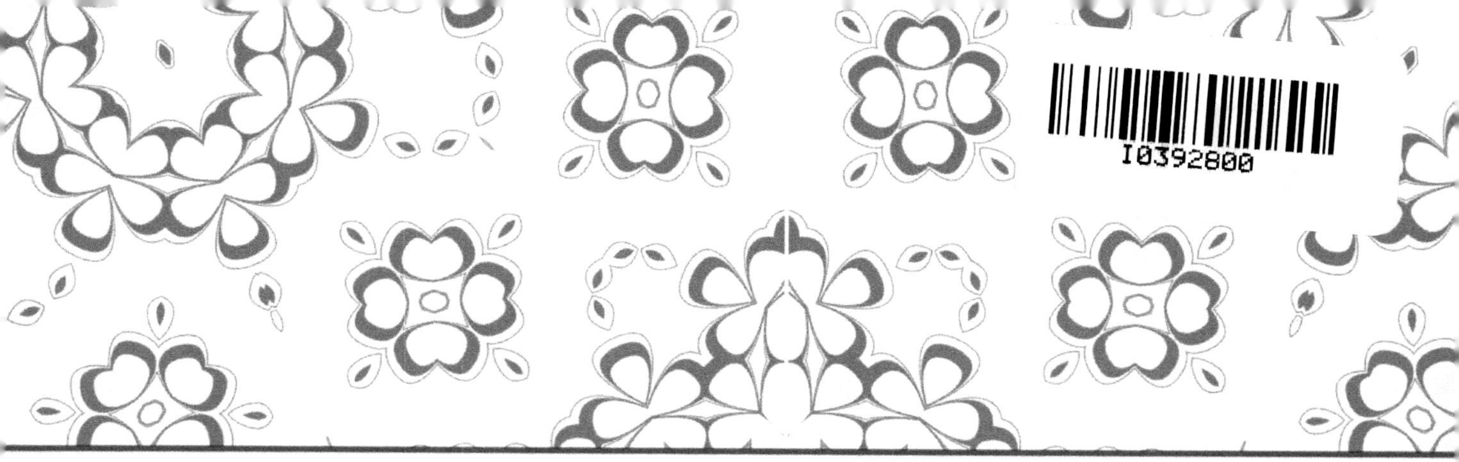

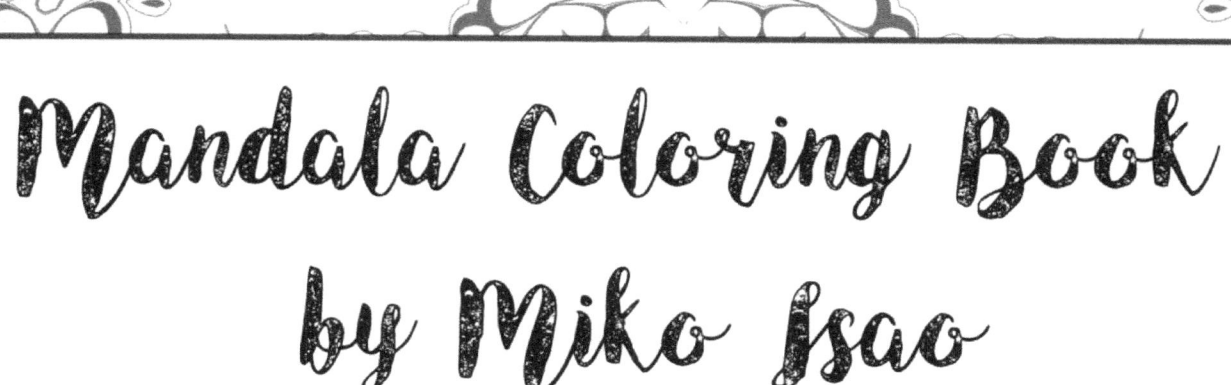

Mandala Coloring Book
by Miko Isao

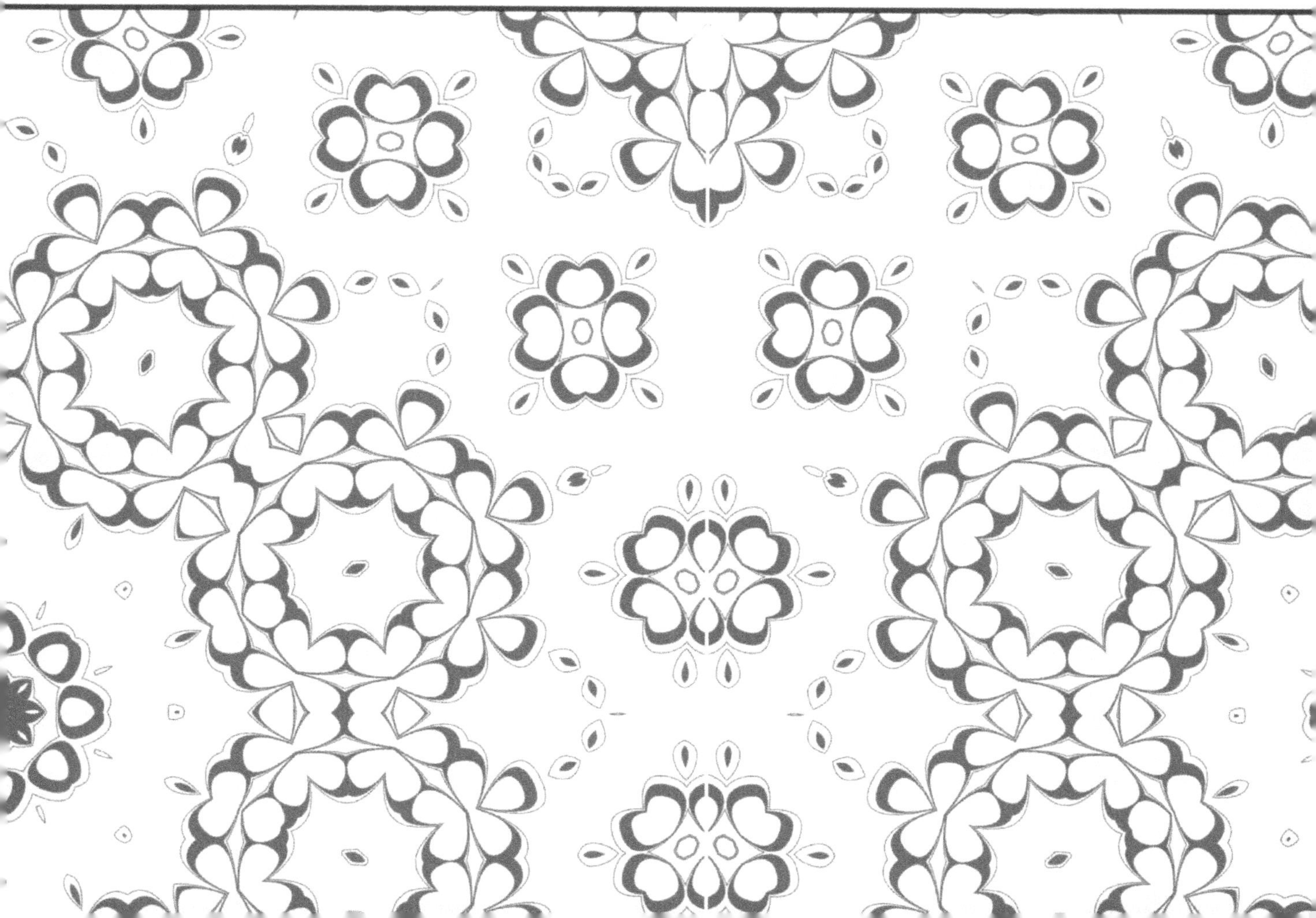

Mandala Coloring Book
By Miko Isao

Copyright: Published in the United States by Miko Isao
Published July 2016

All rights reserved. No part of this publication may be reproduced, stored in retrieval system, copied in any form or by any means, electronic, mechanical, photocopying, recording or otherwise transmitted without written permission from the publisher. Please do not participate in or encourage piracy of this material in any way. You must not circulate this book in any format. Miko Isao *does not control or direct users' actions and is not responsible for the information or content shared, harm and/or actions of the book readers.*

ISBN-13: 978-1535418812

ISBN-10: 1535418818

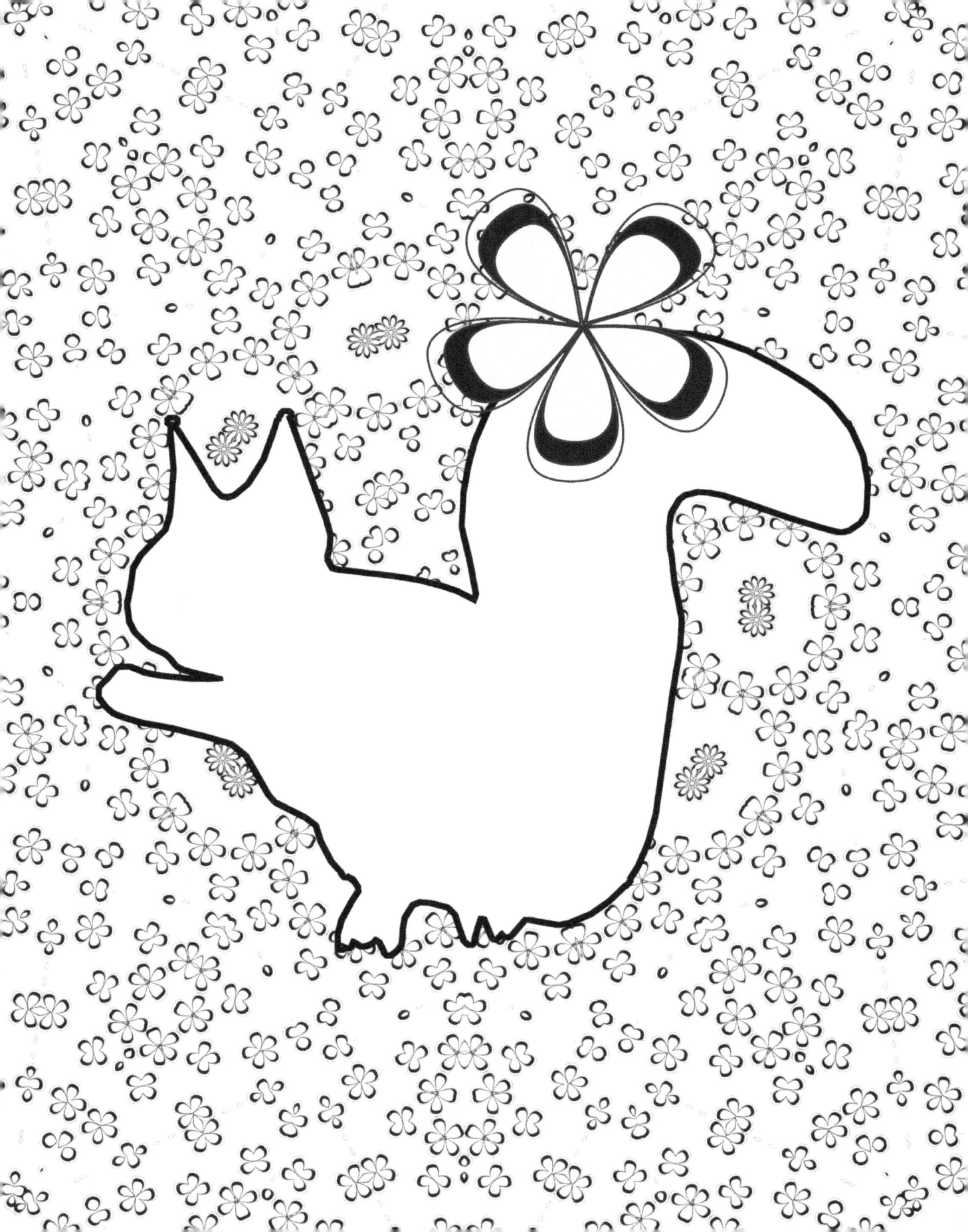

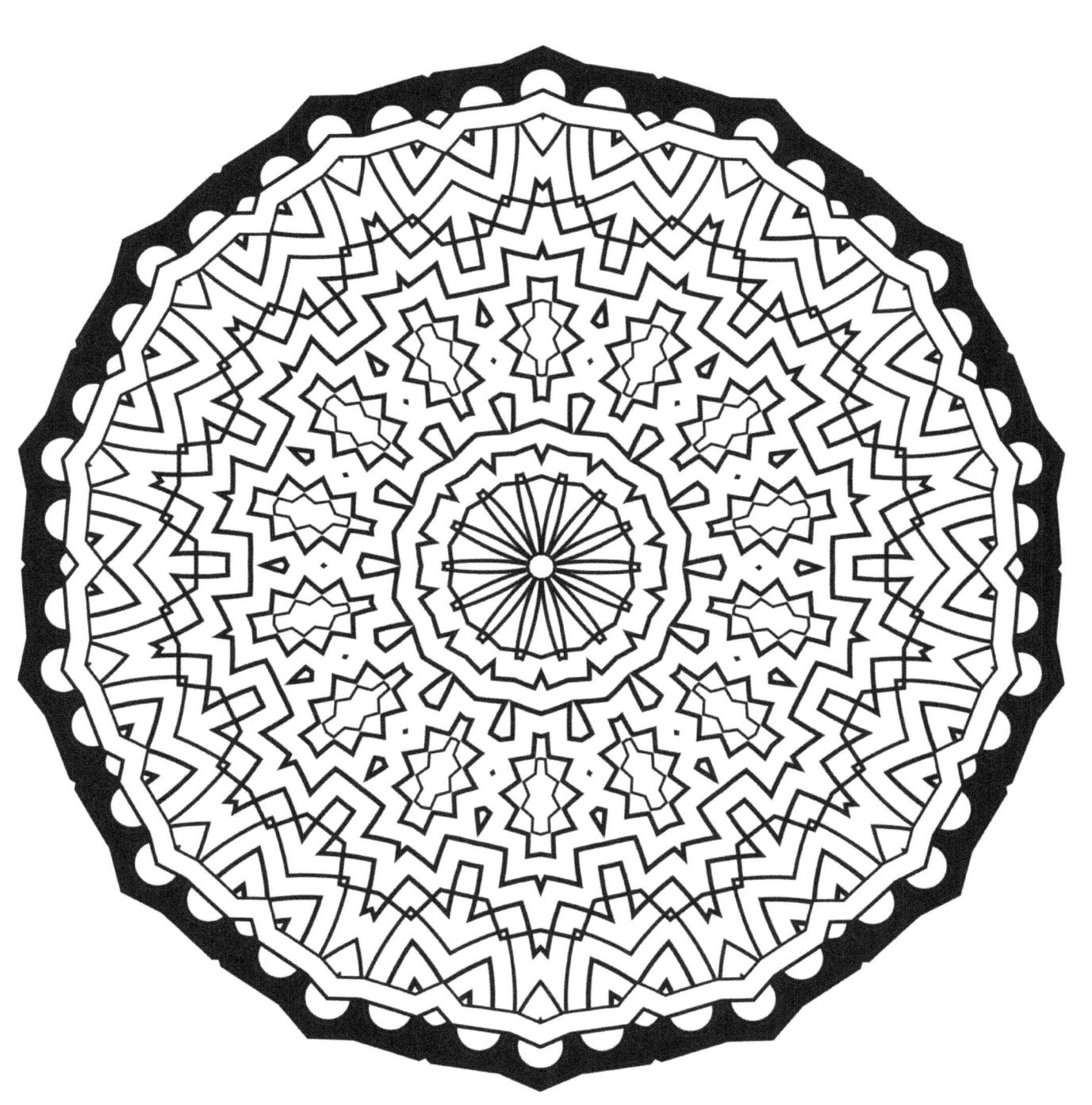

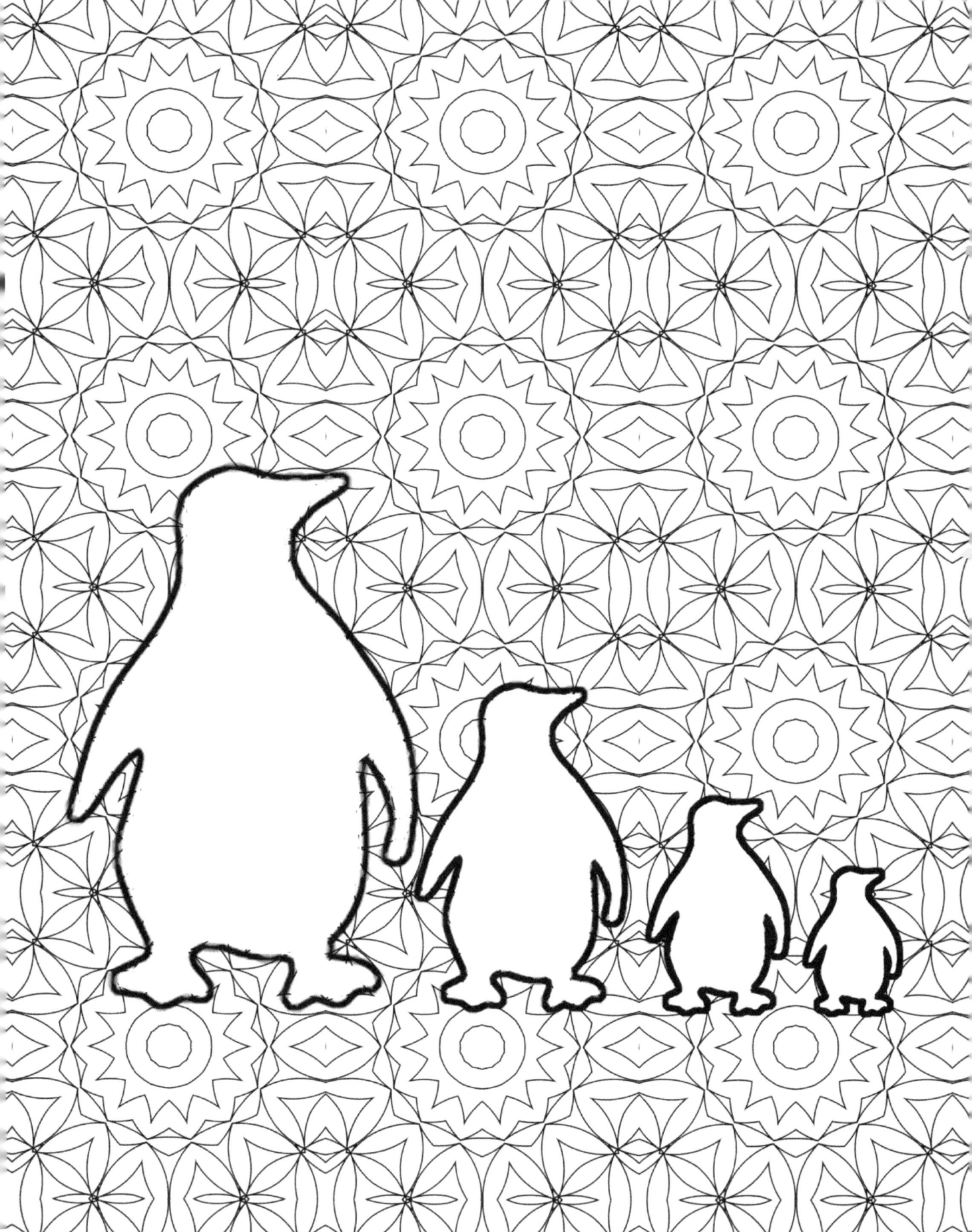

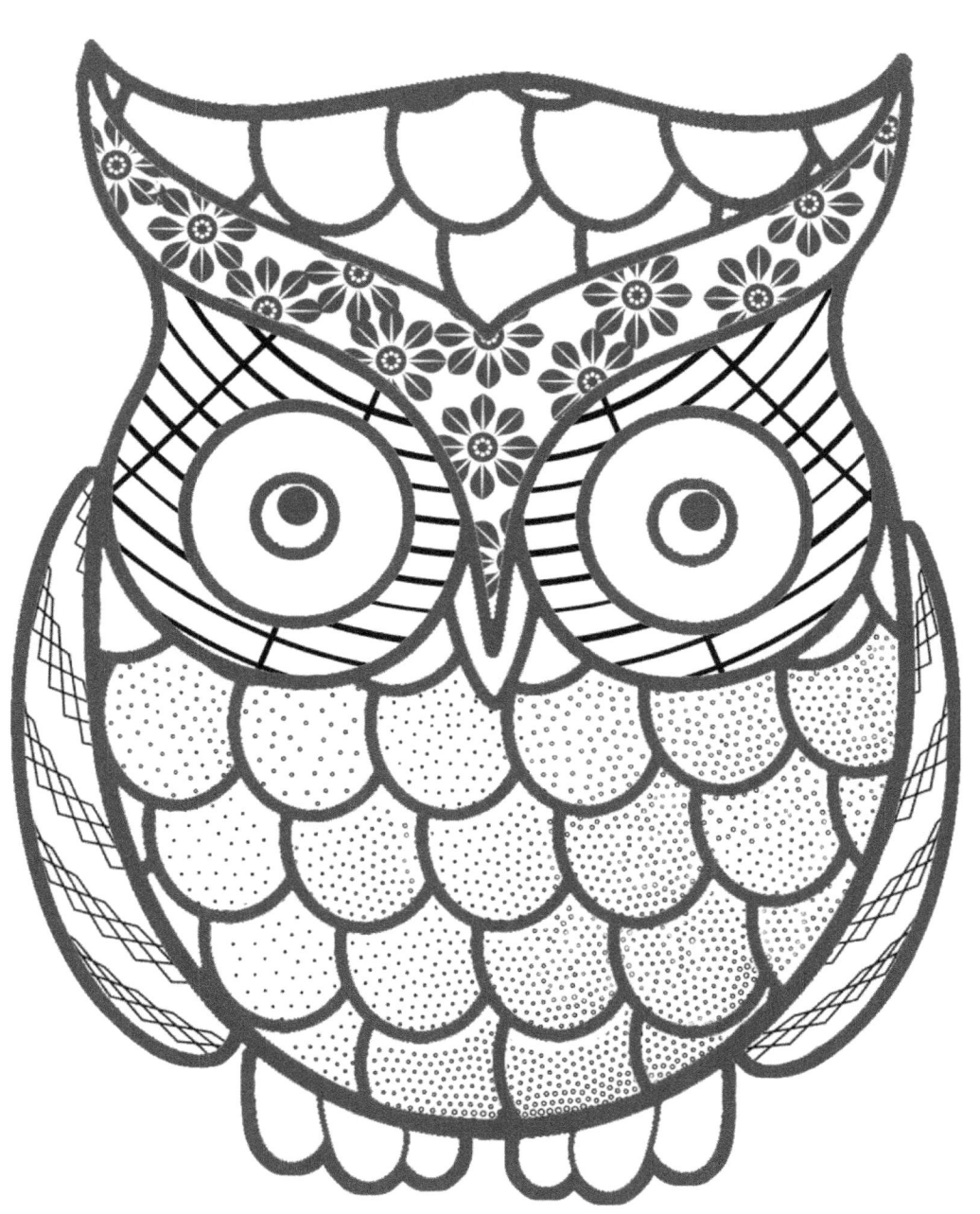

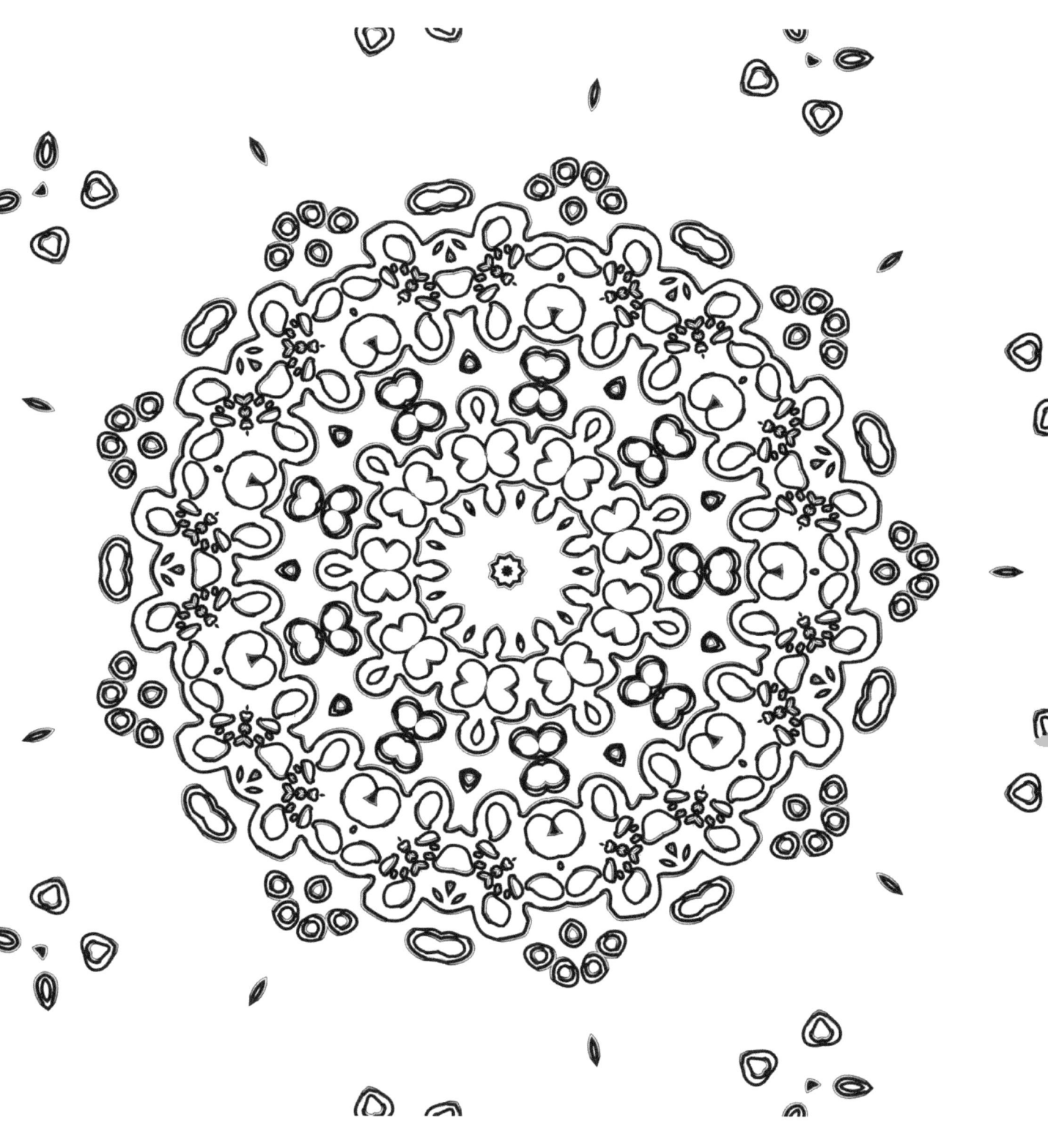

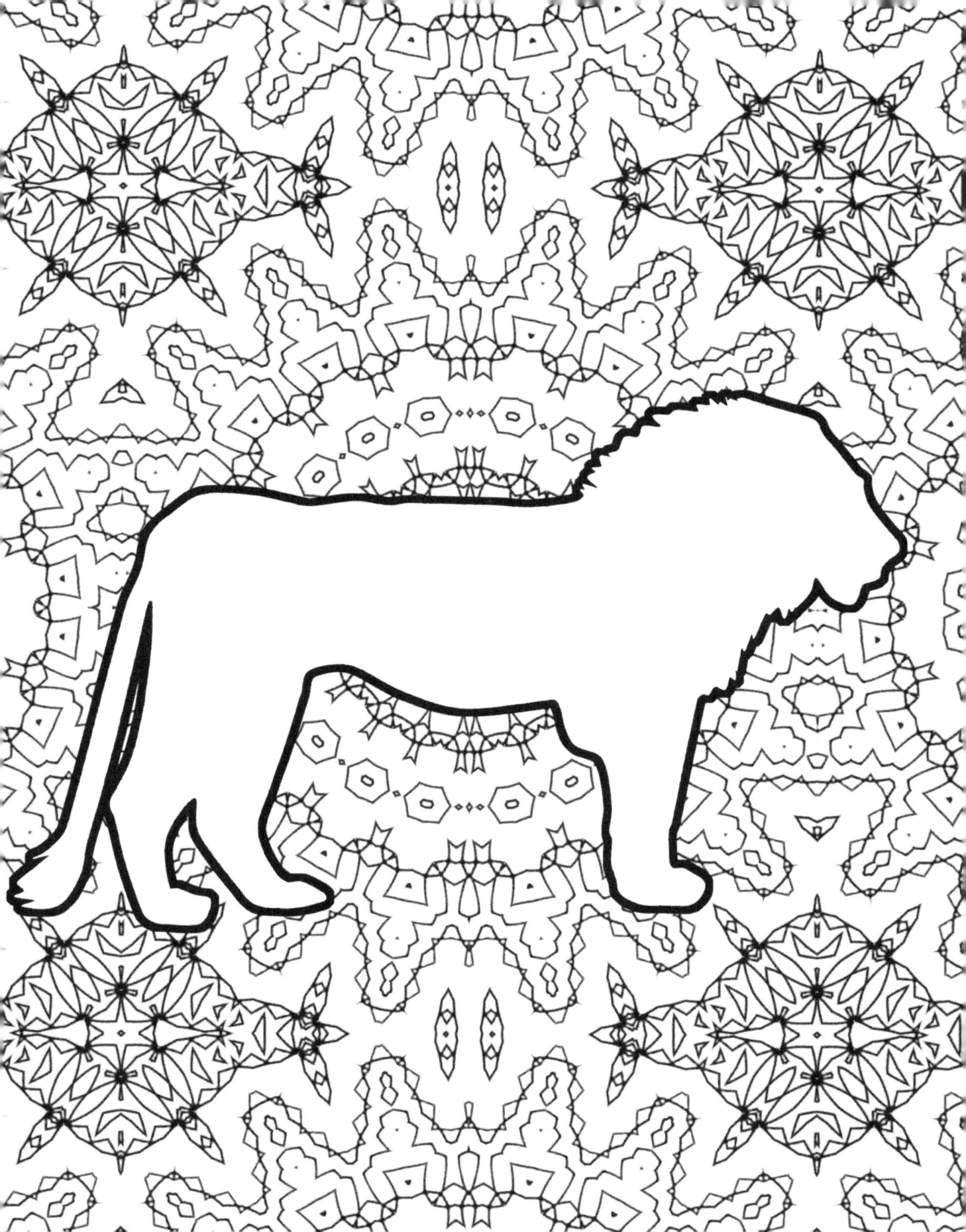

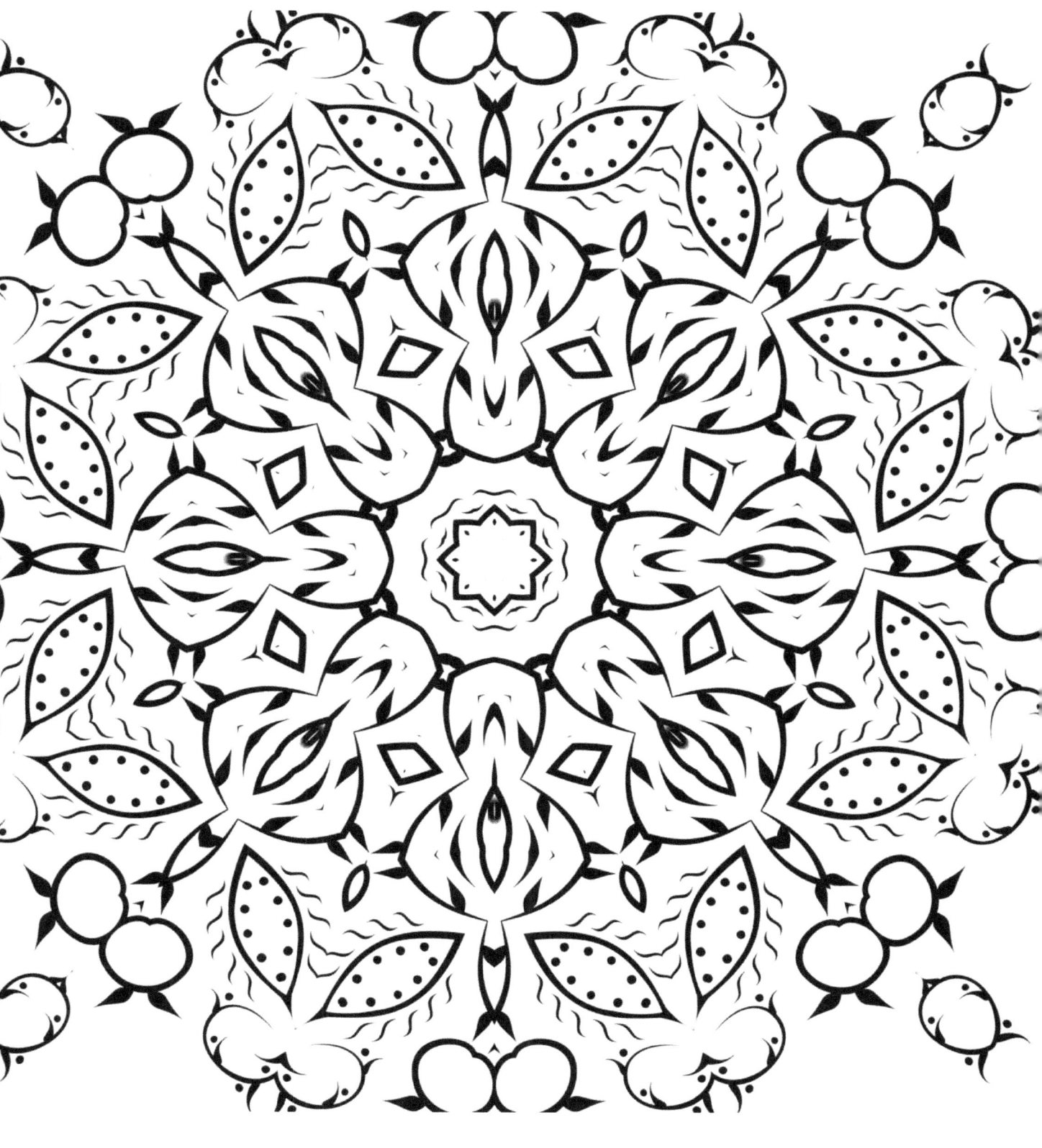

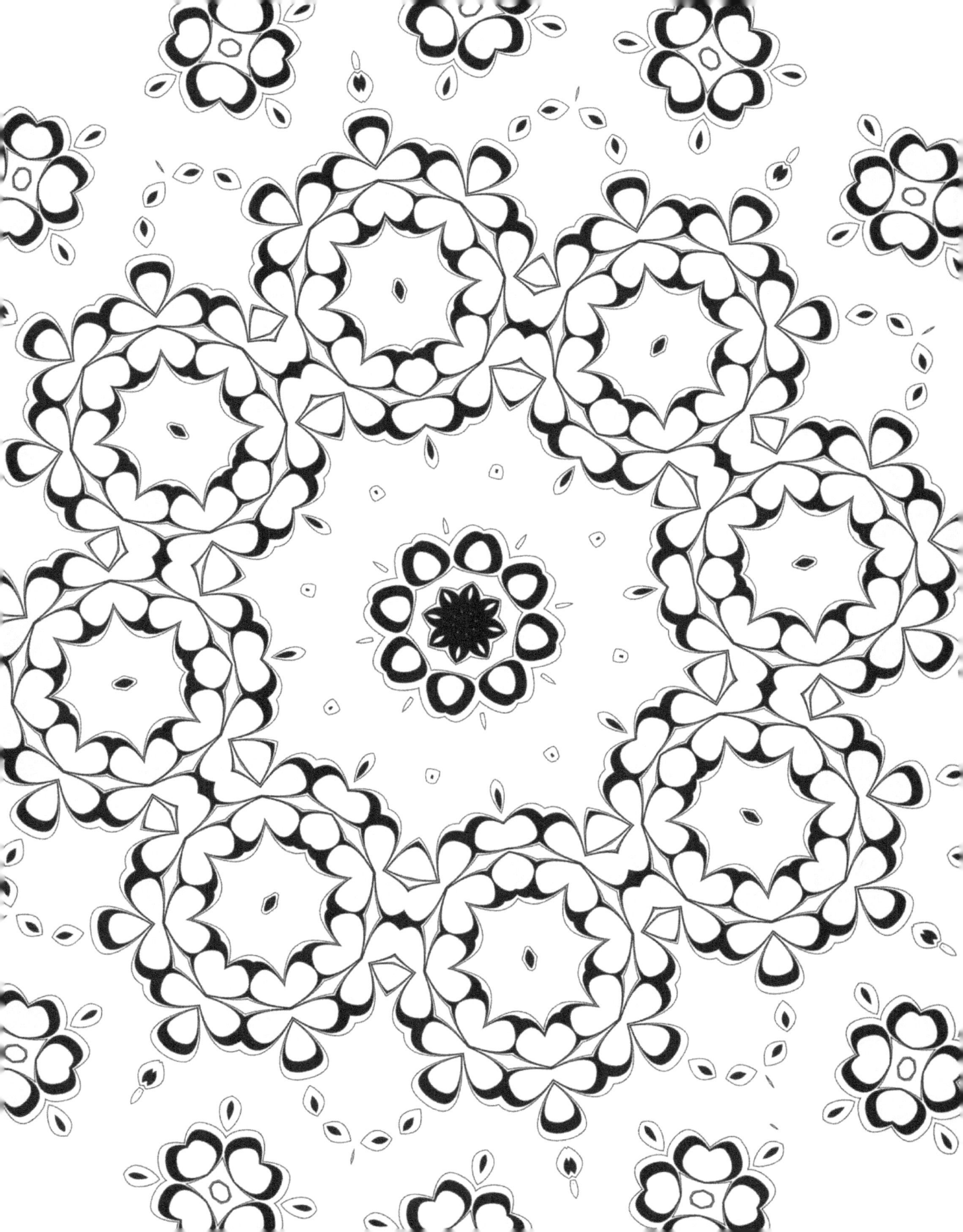

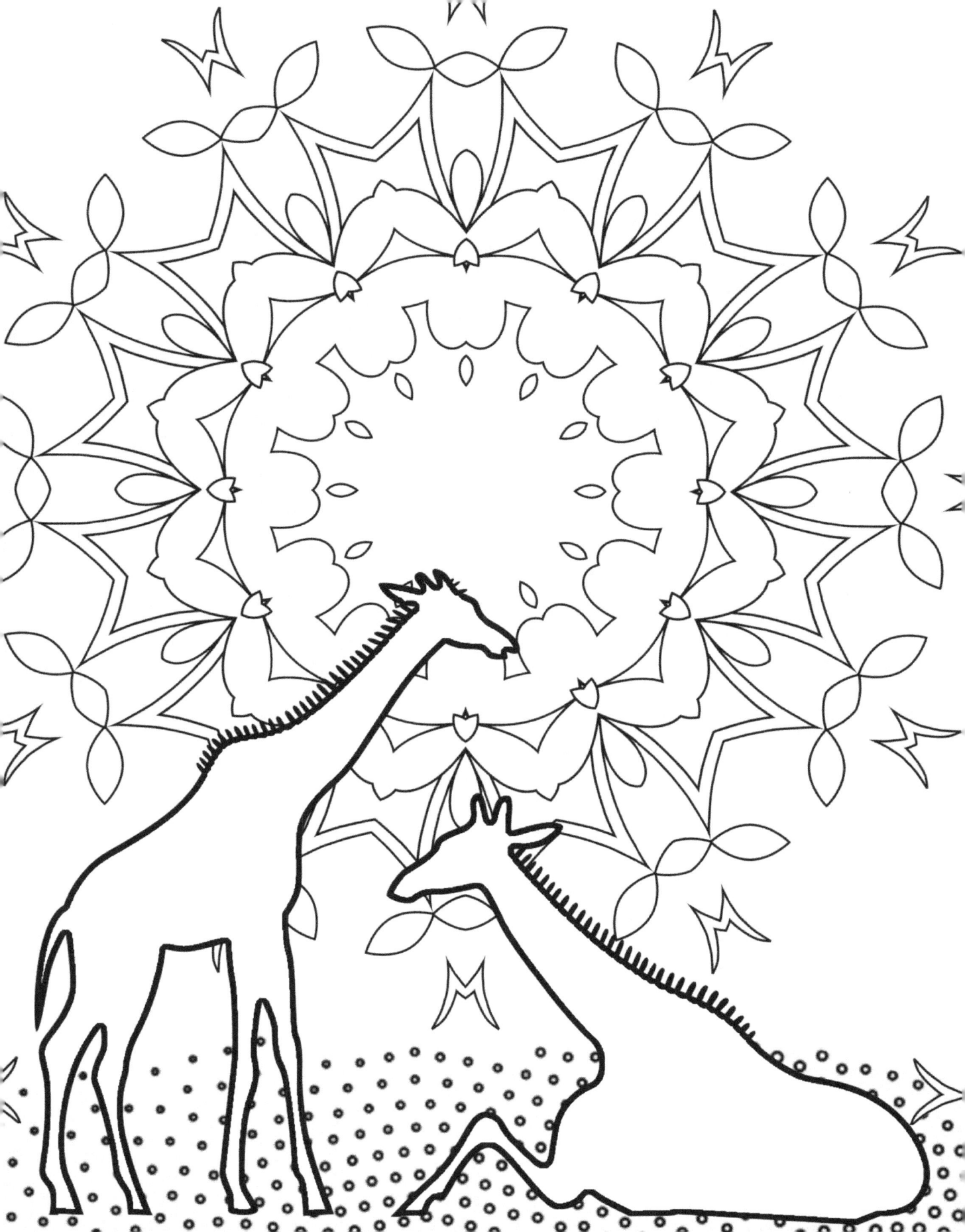

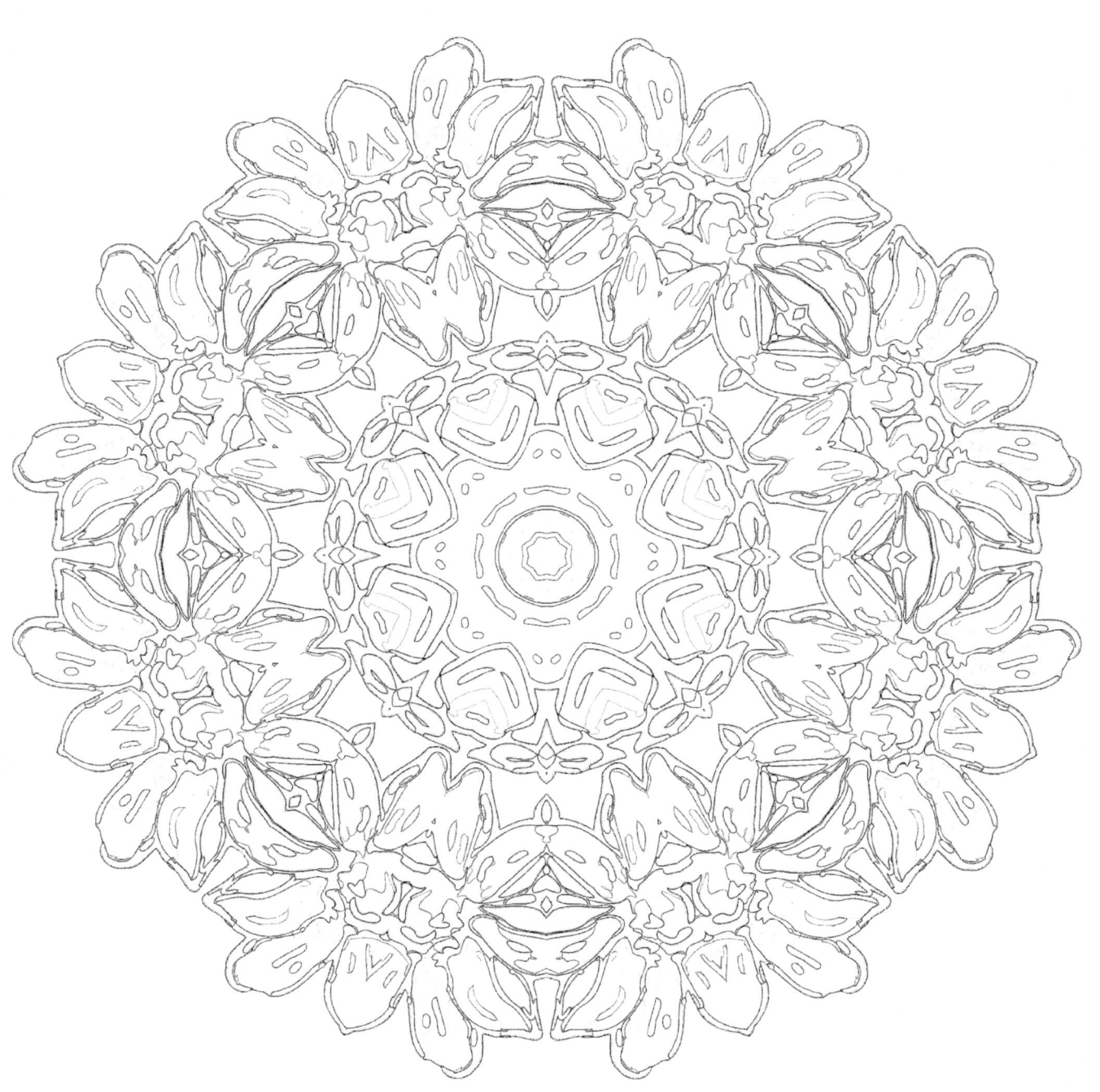

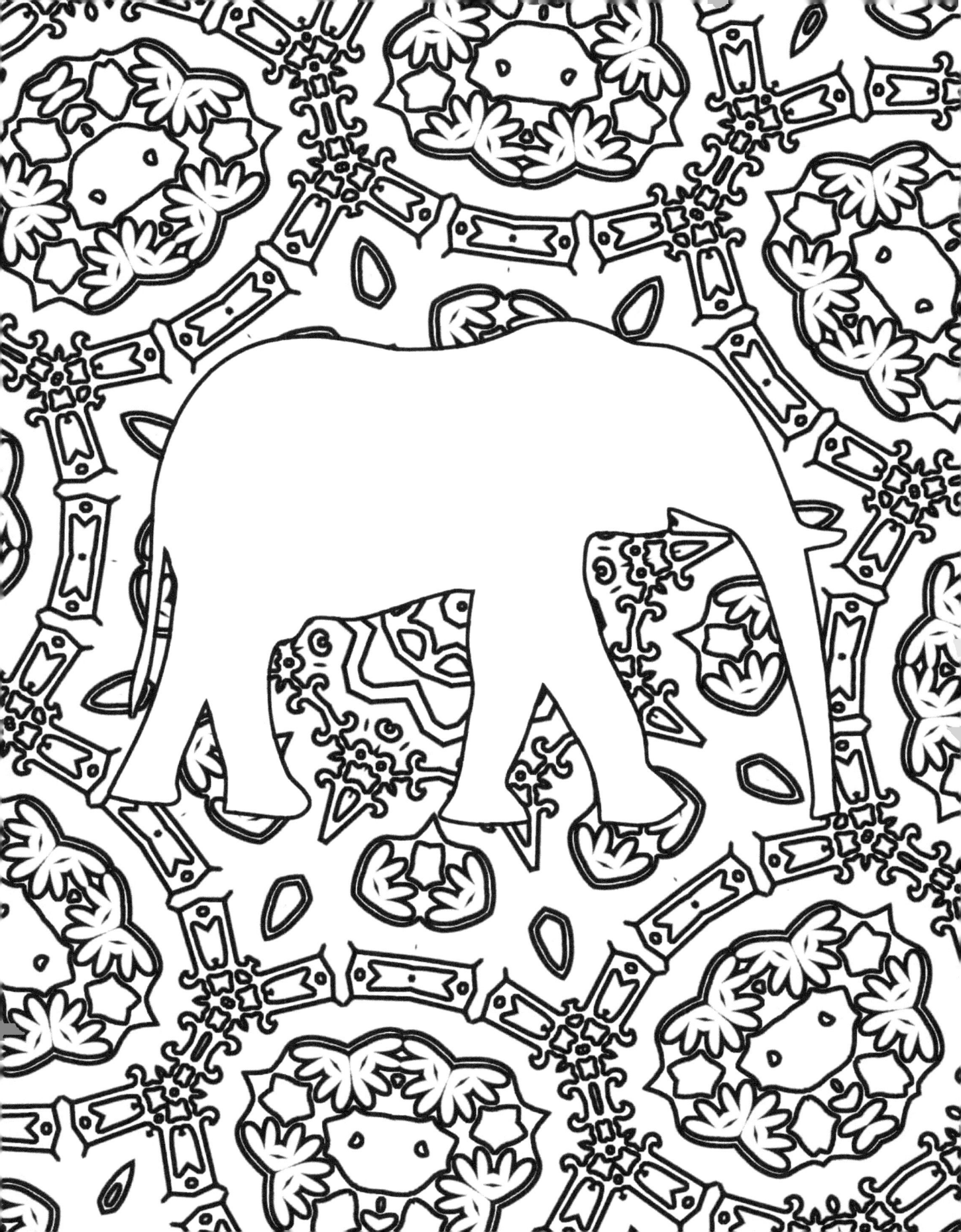

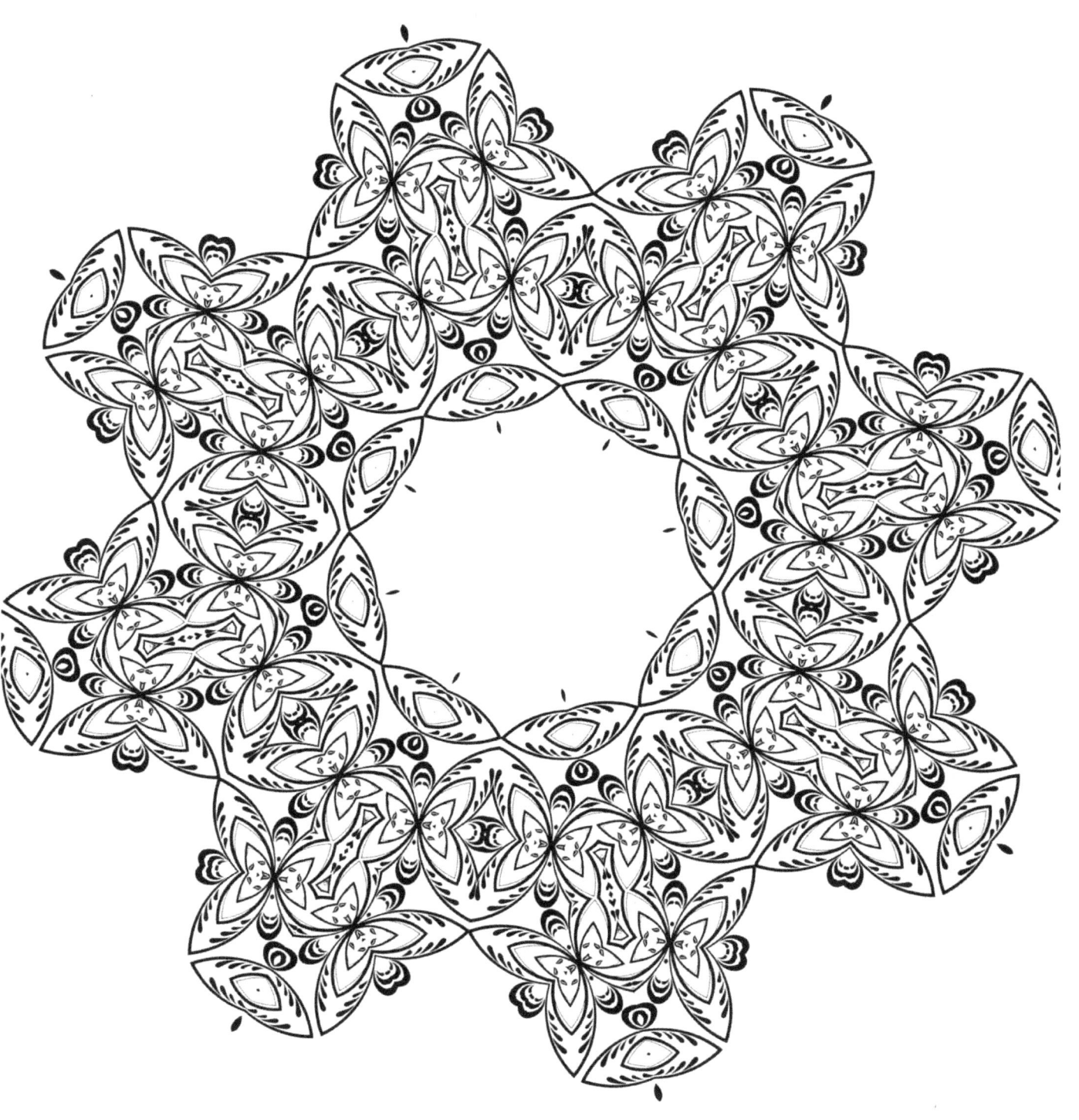

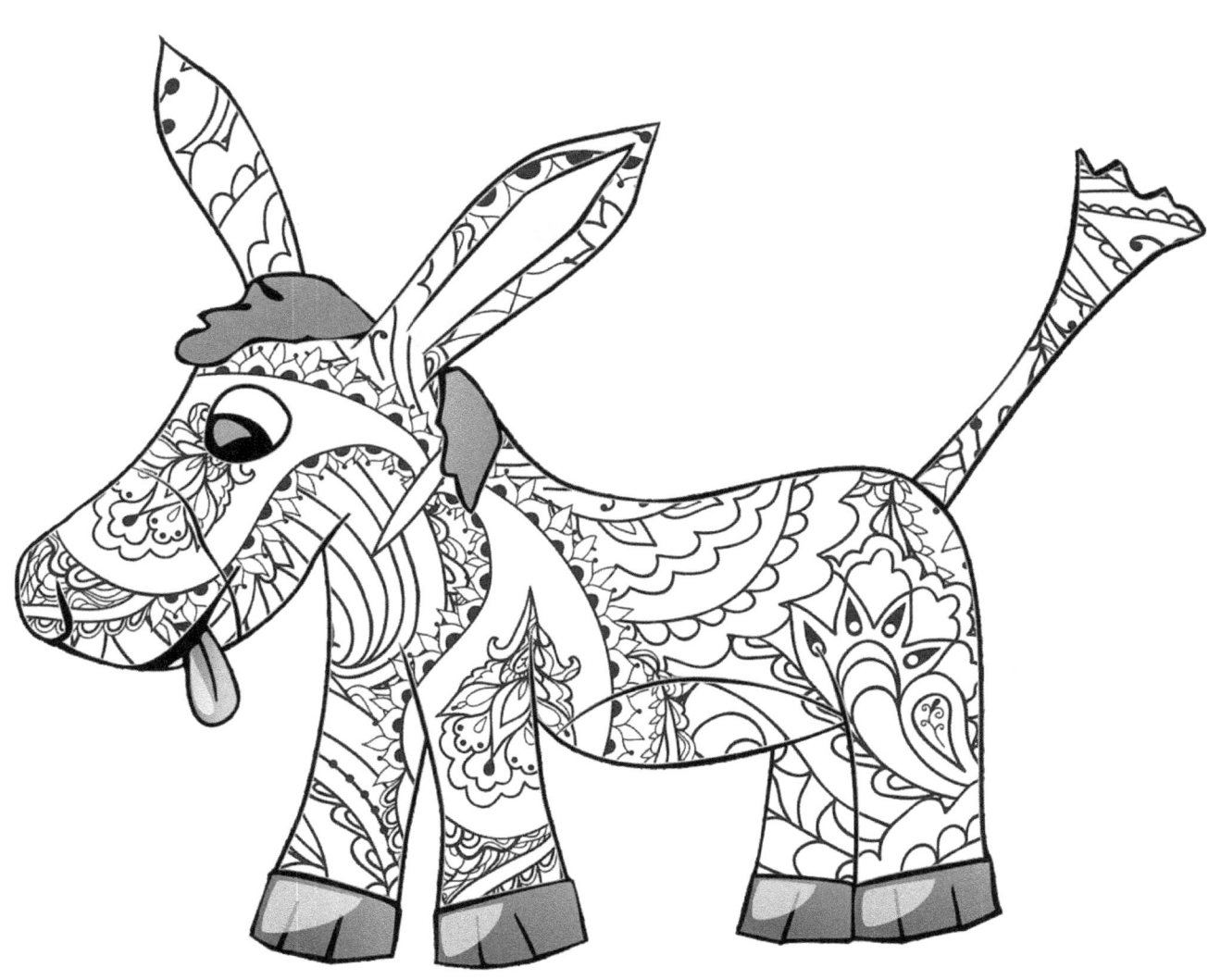

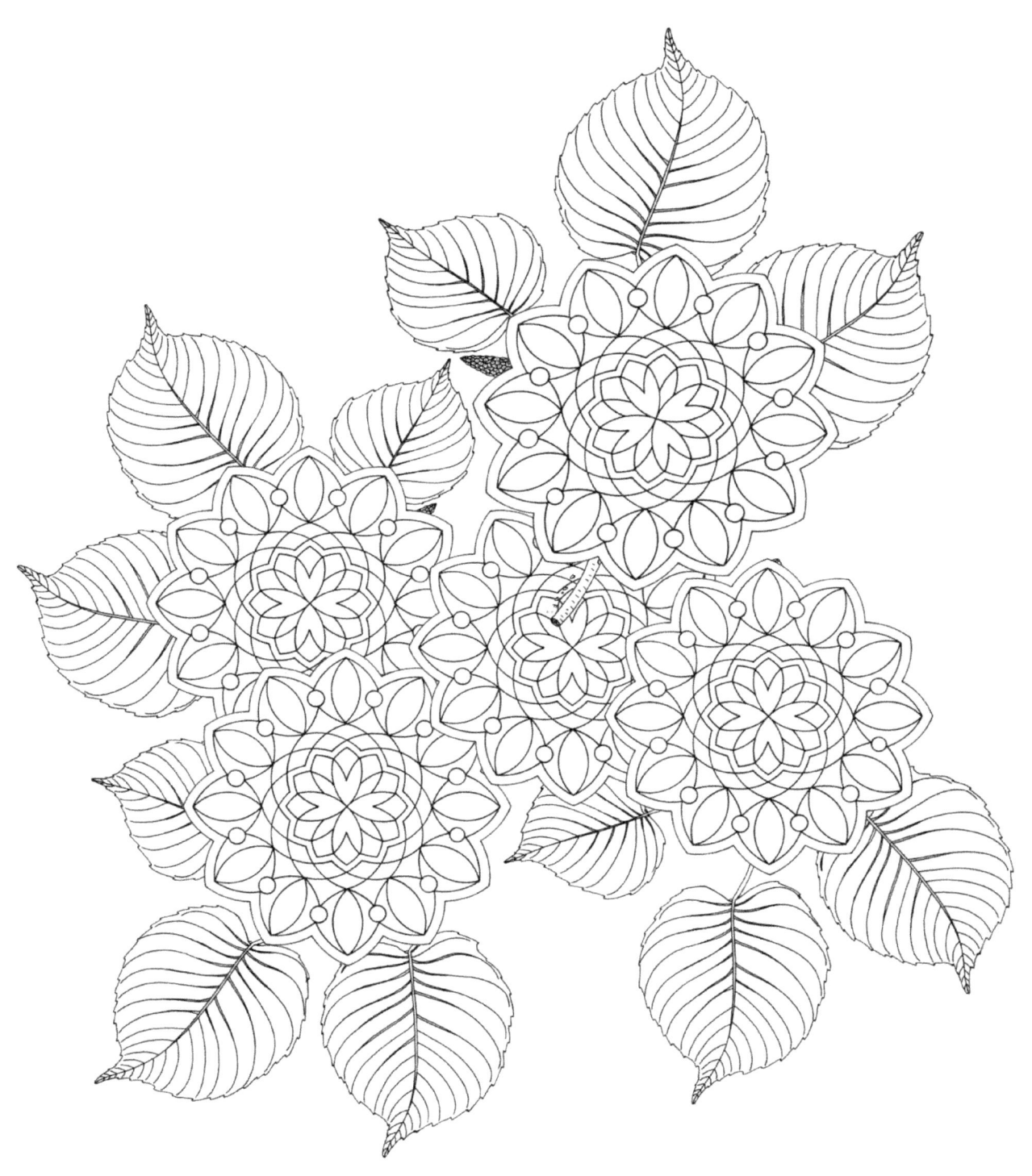

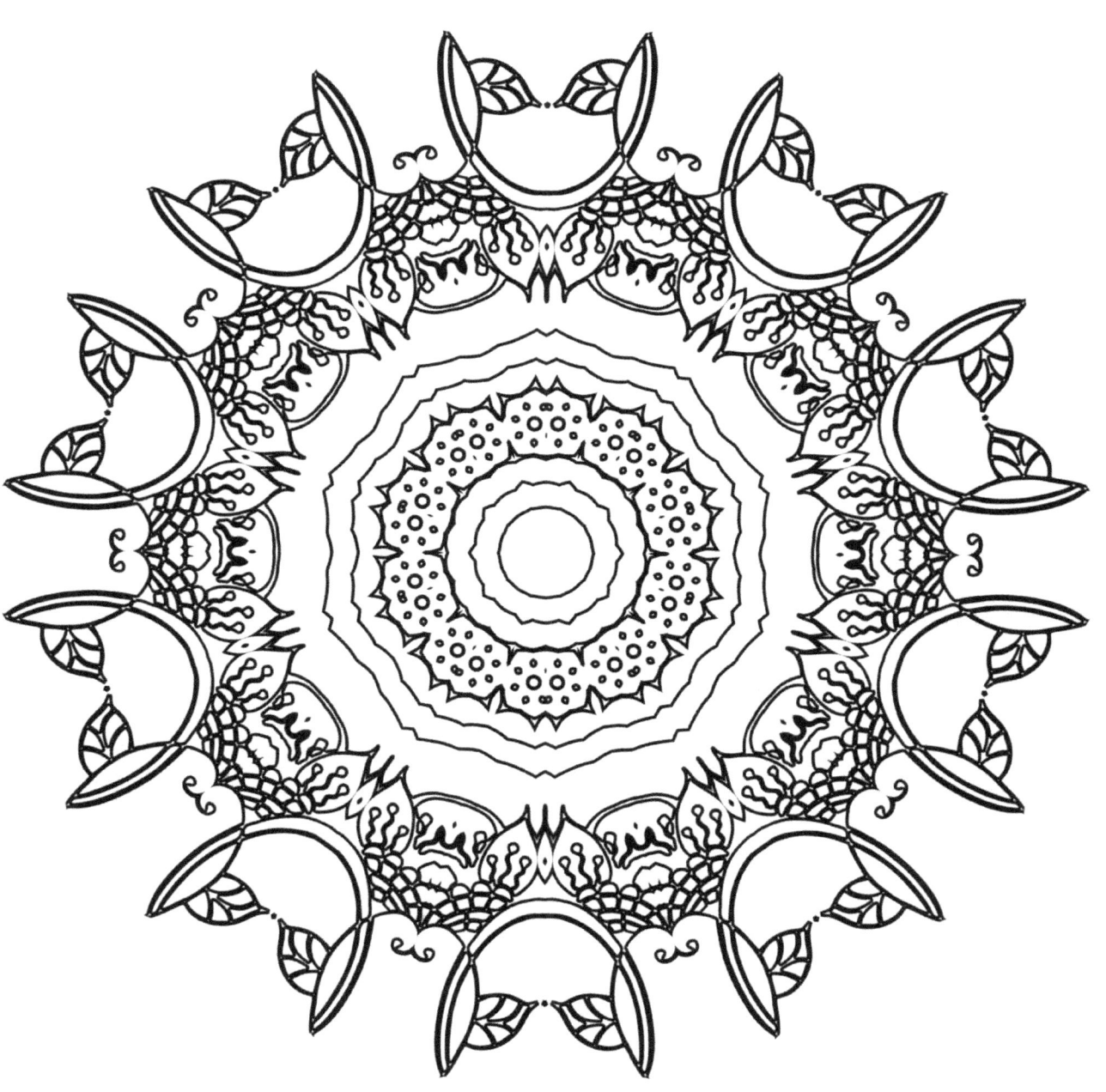

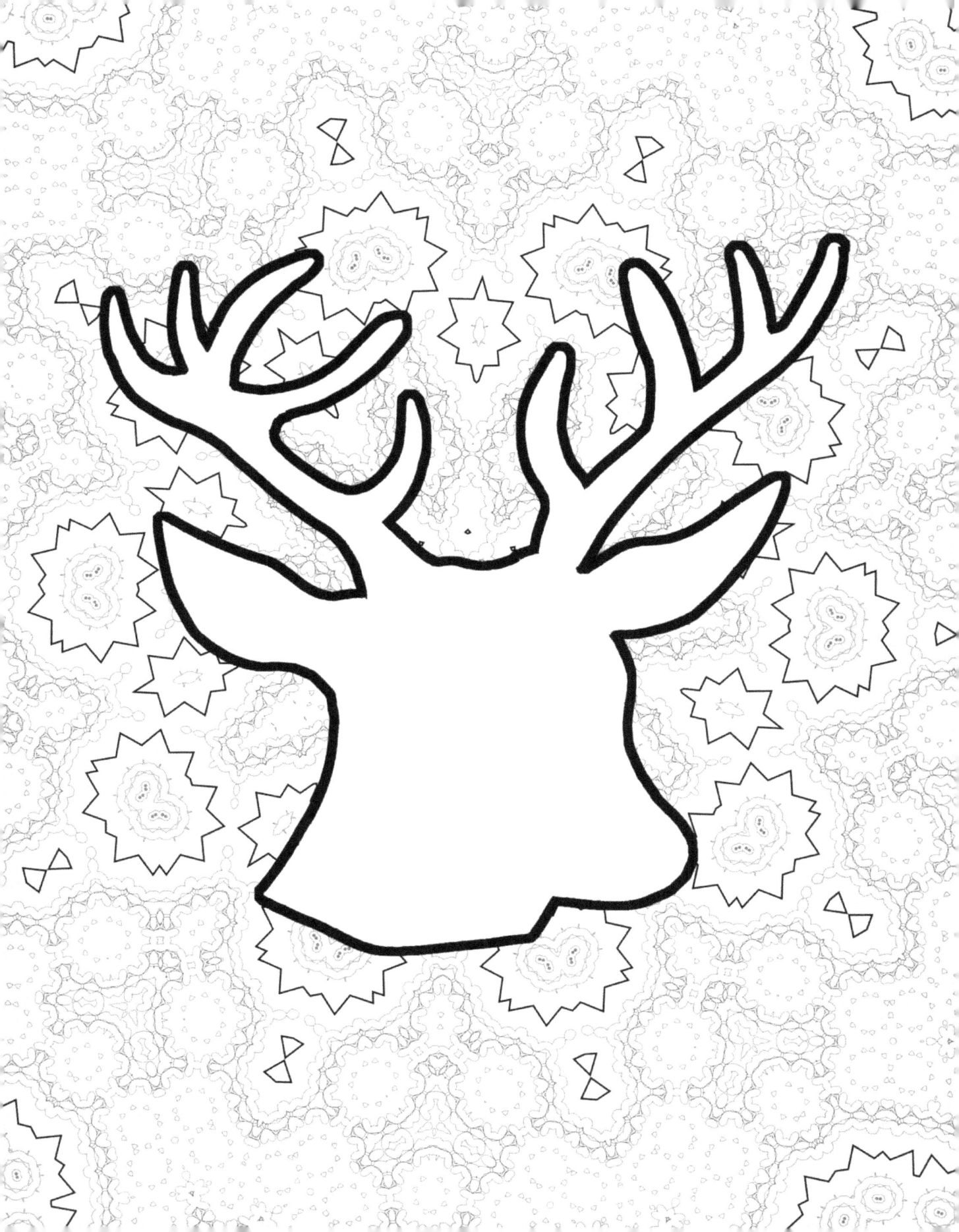

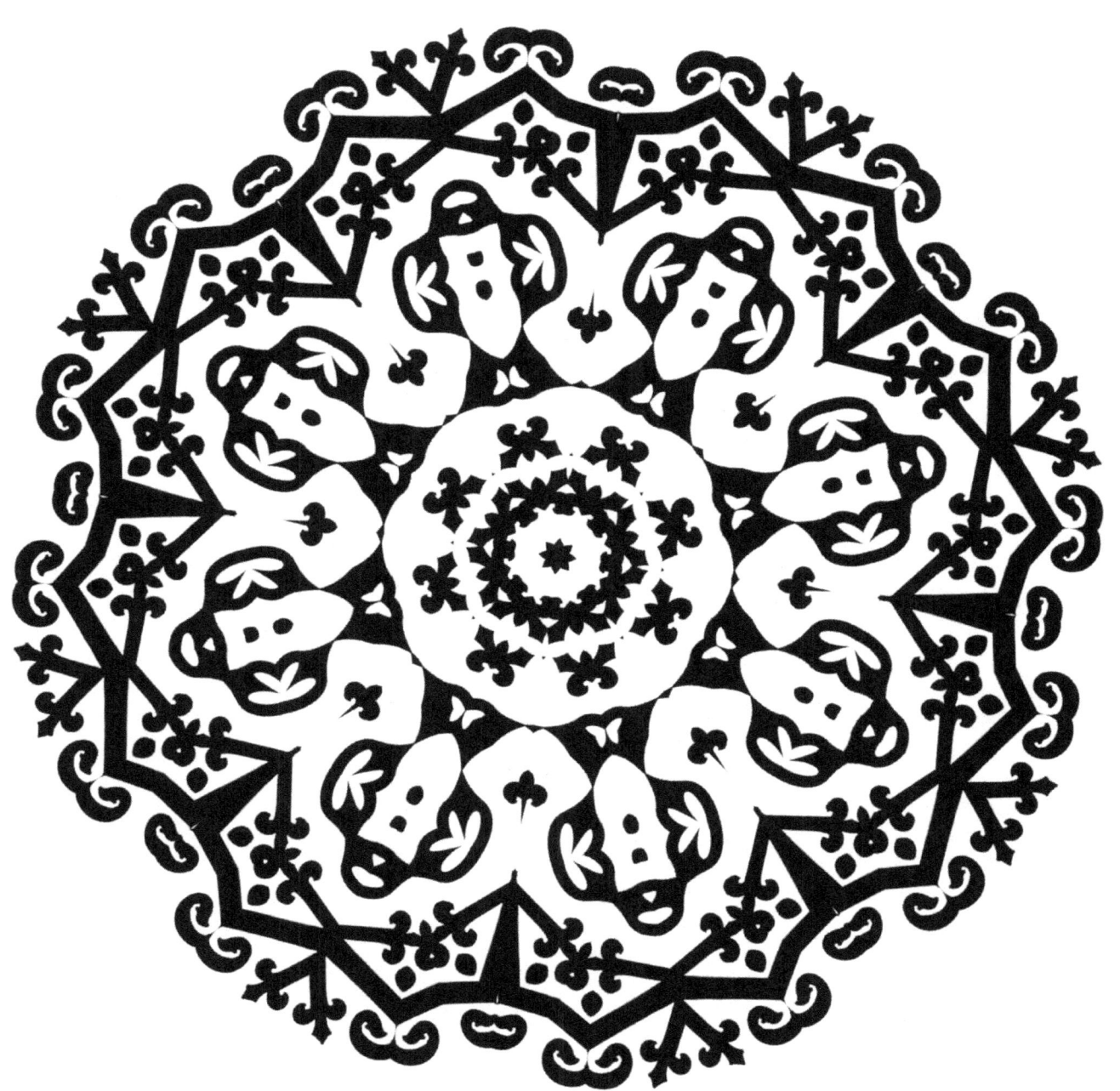

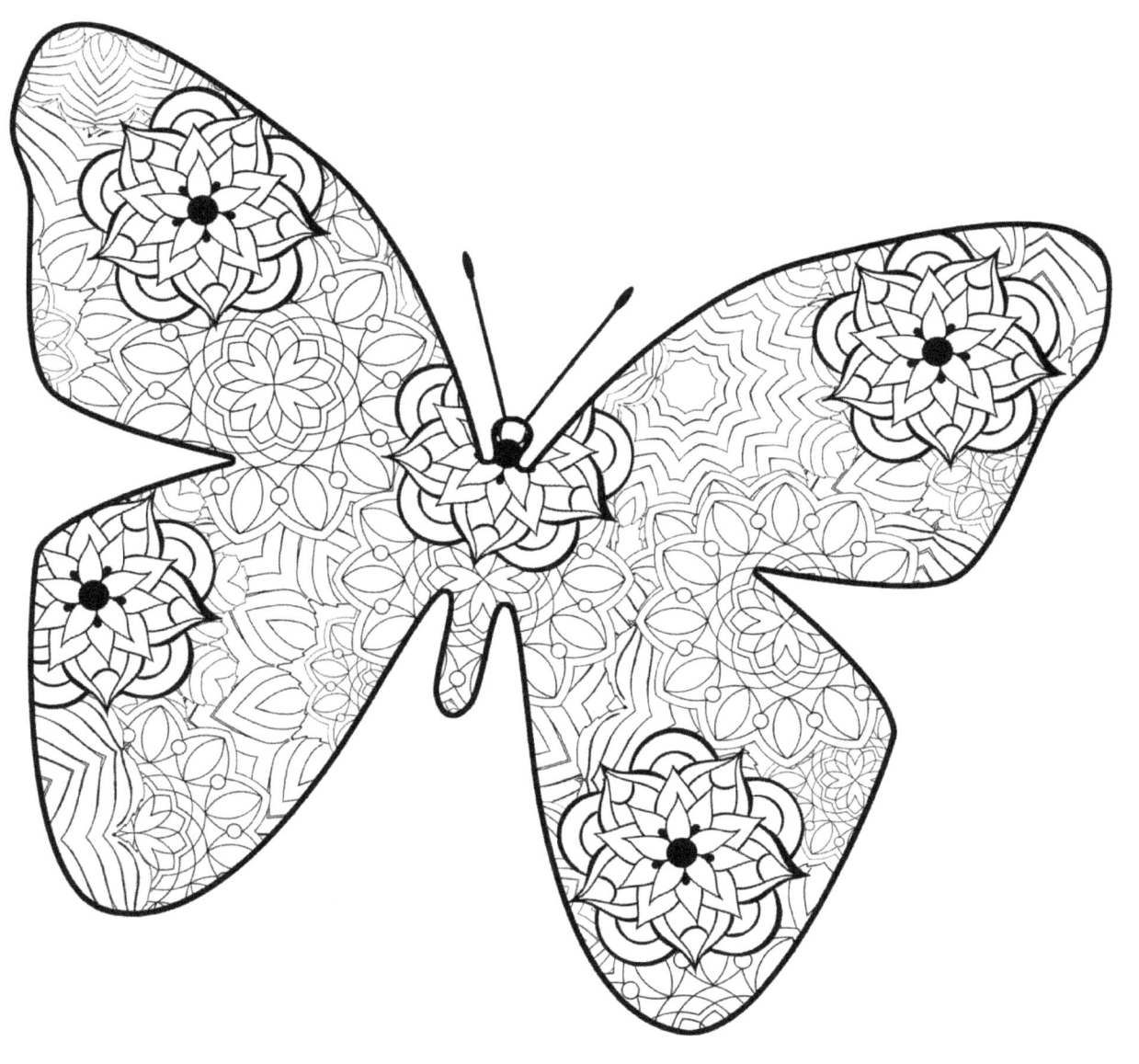

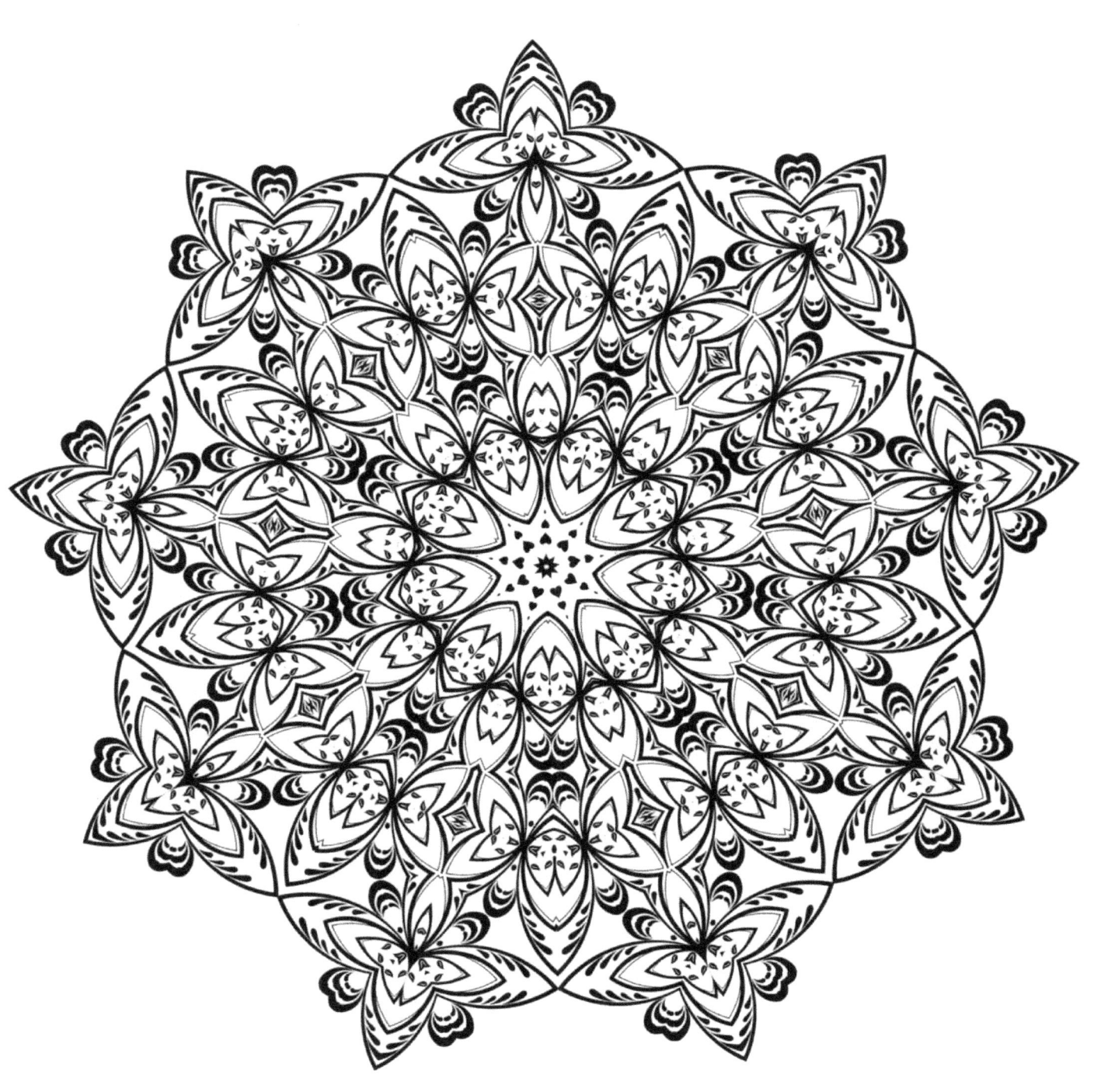

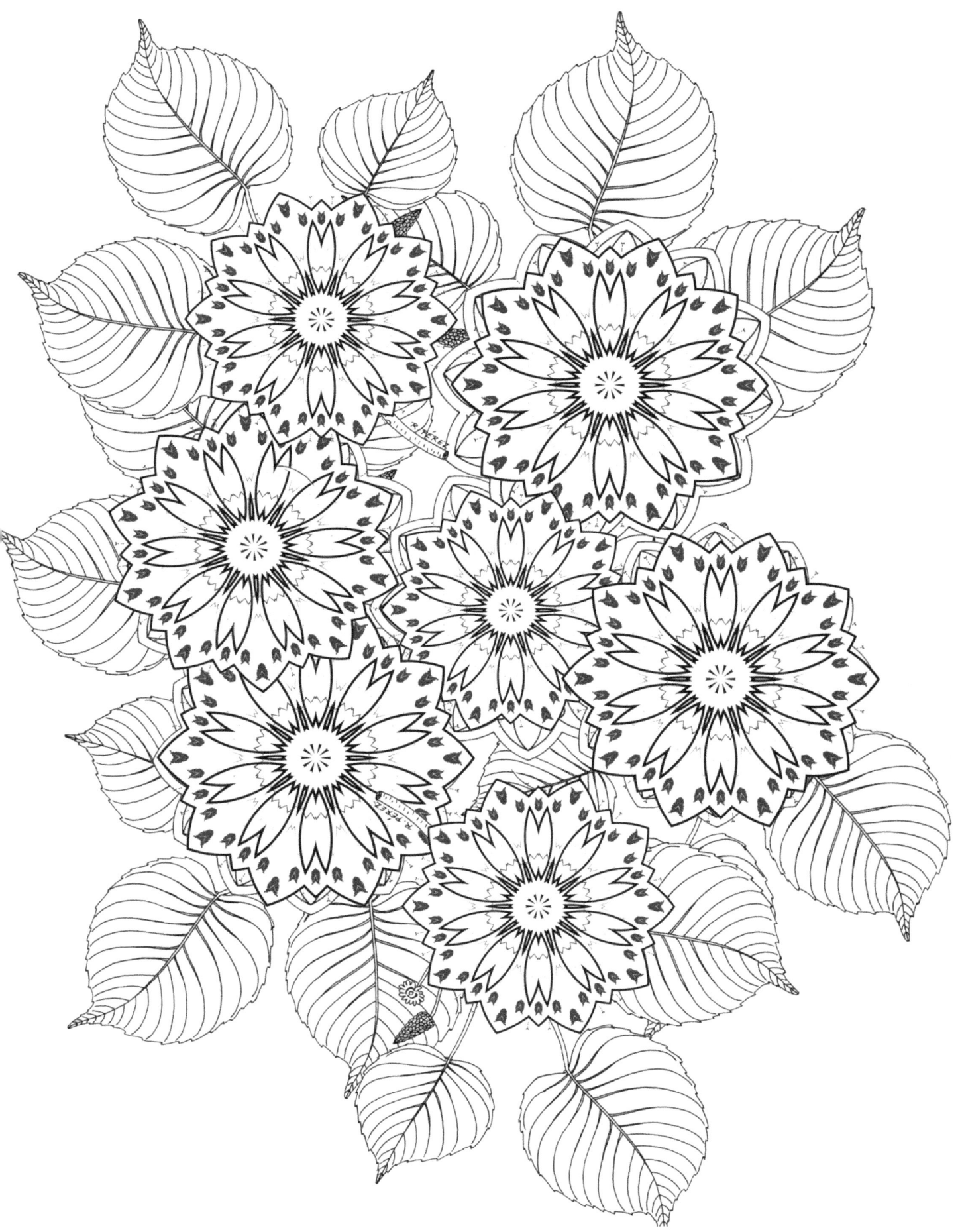

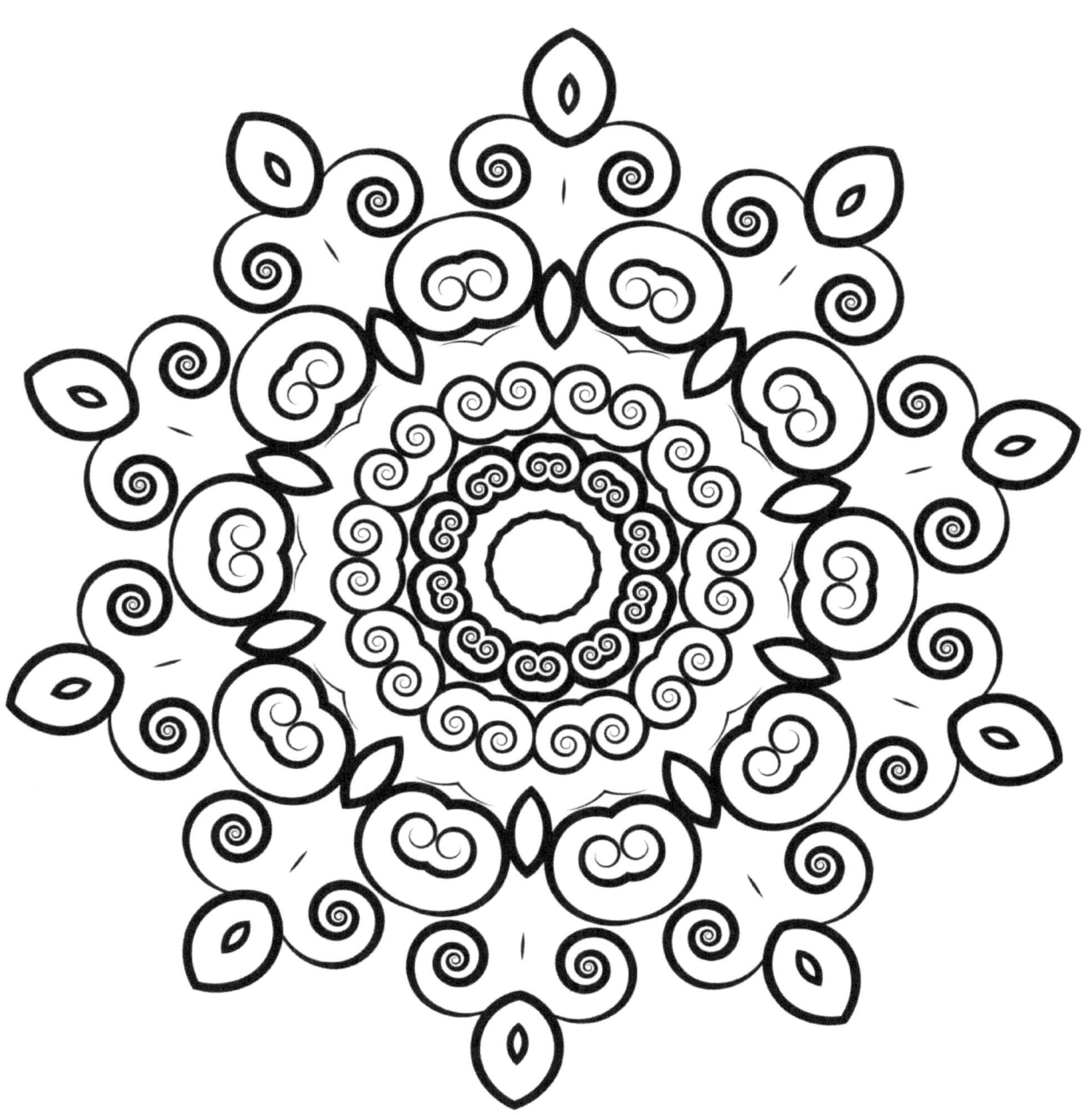

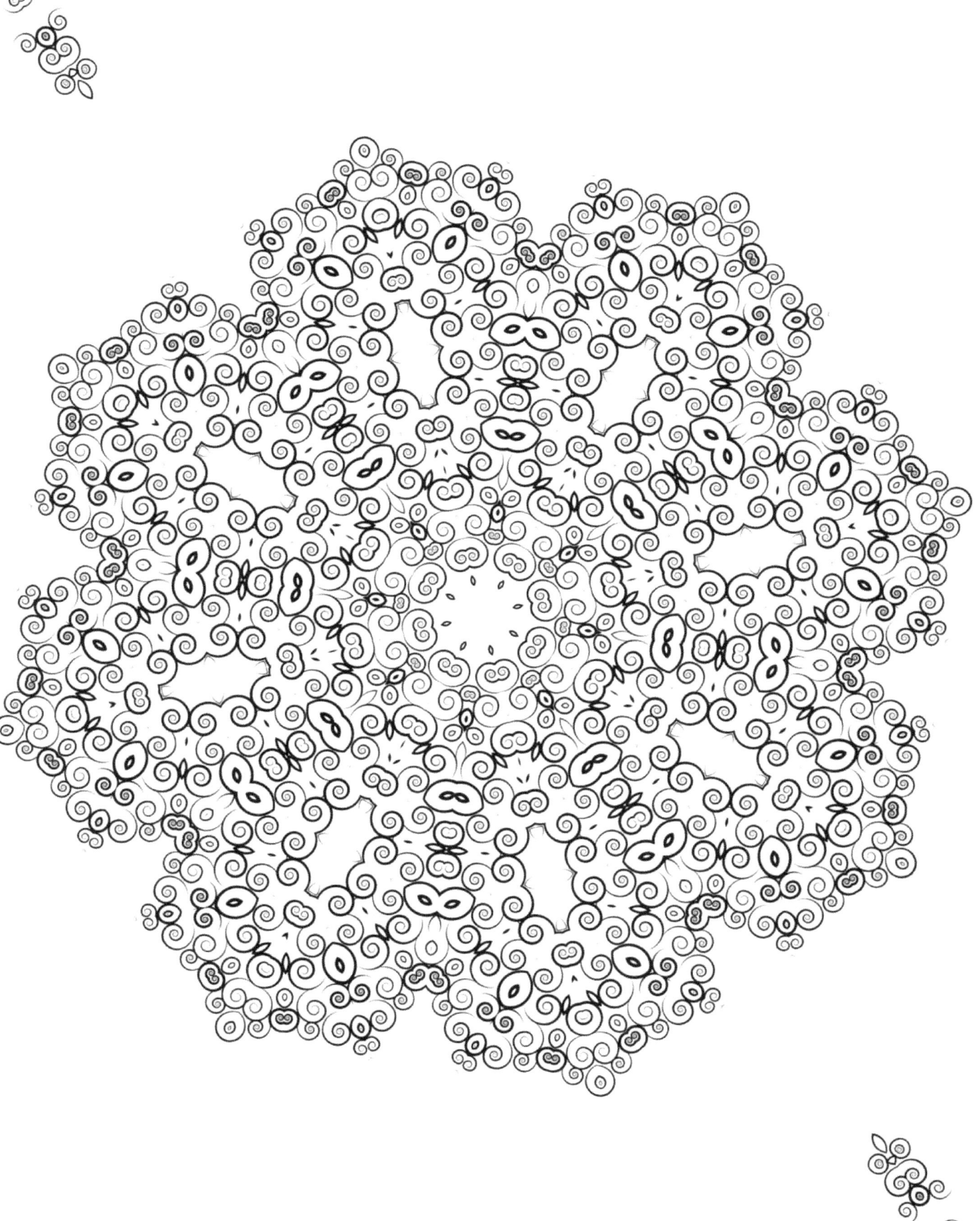

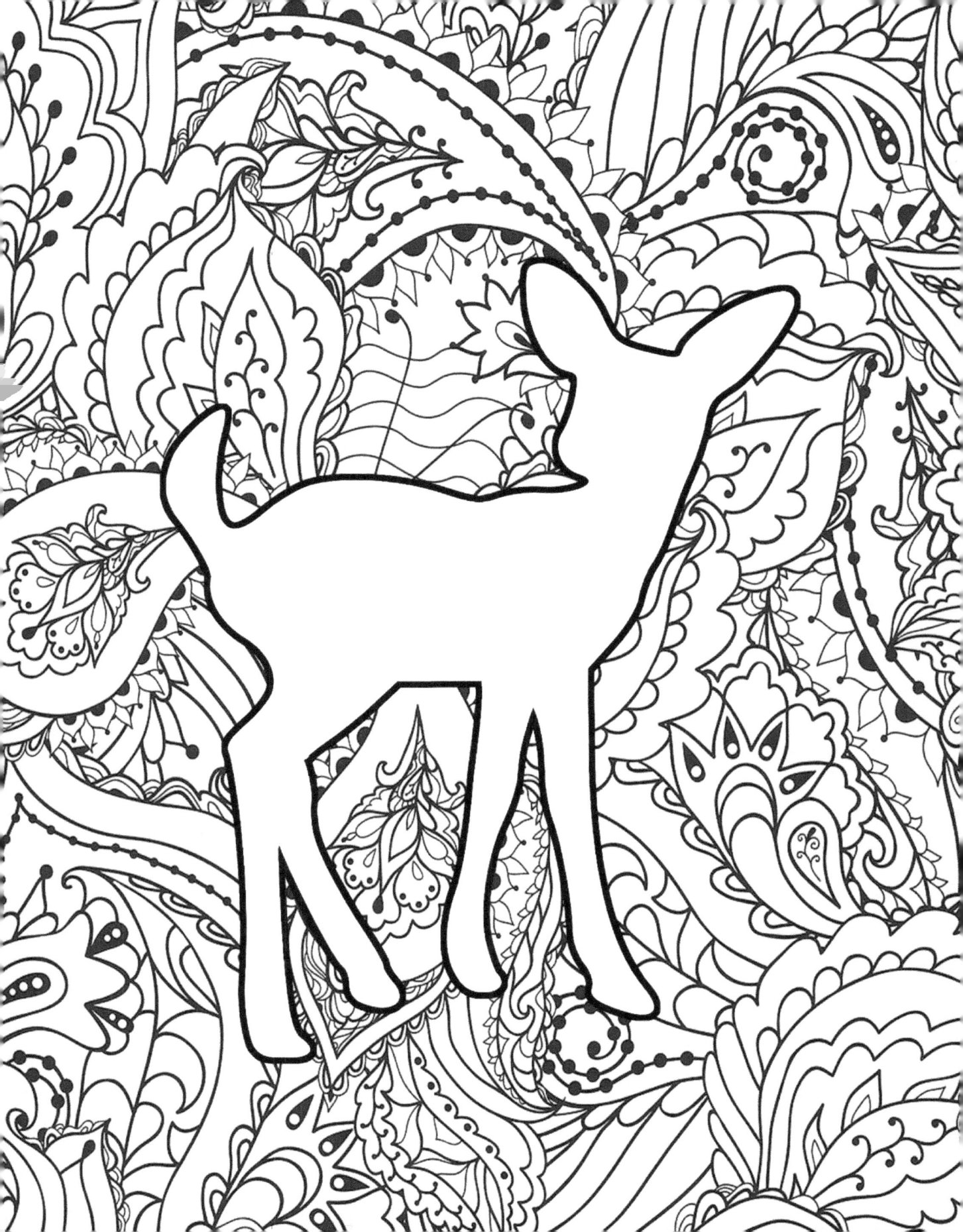

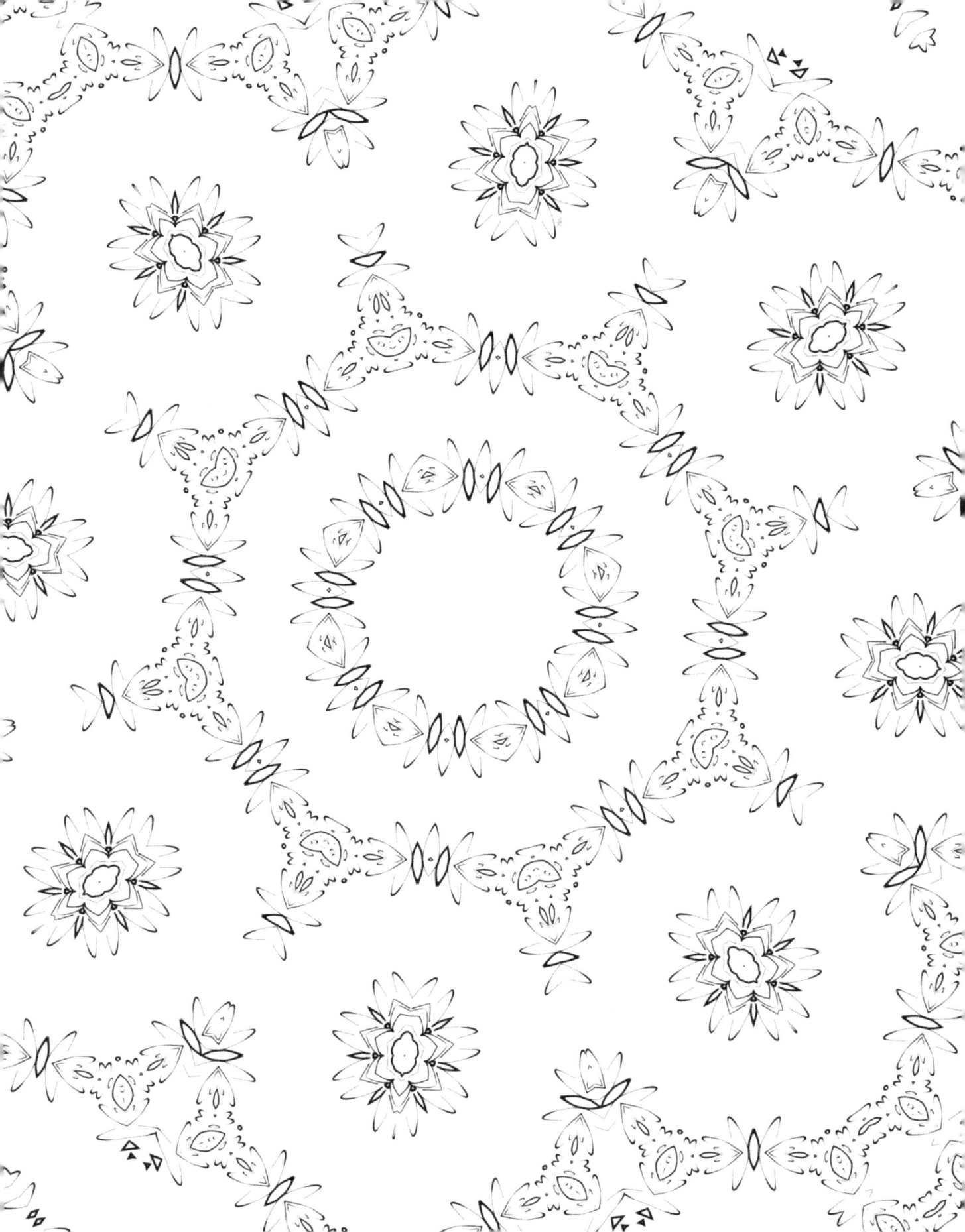

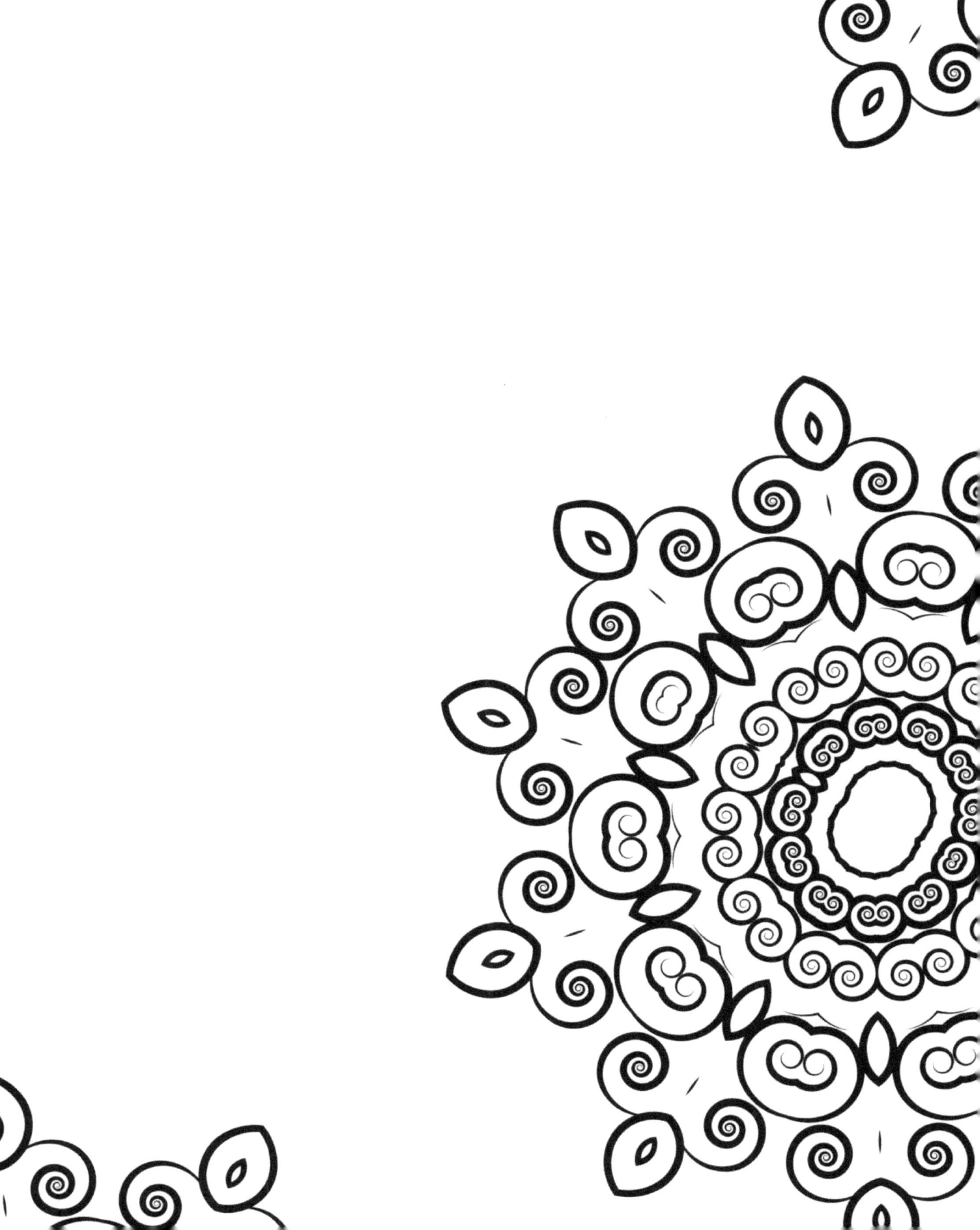

Thank you

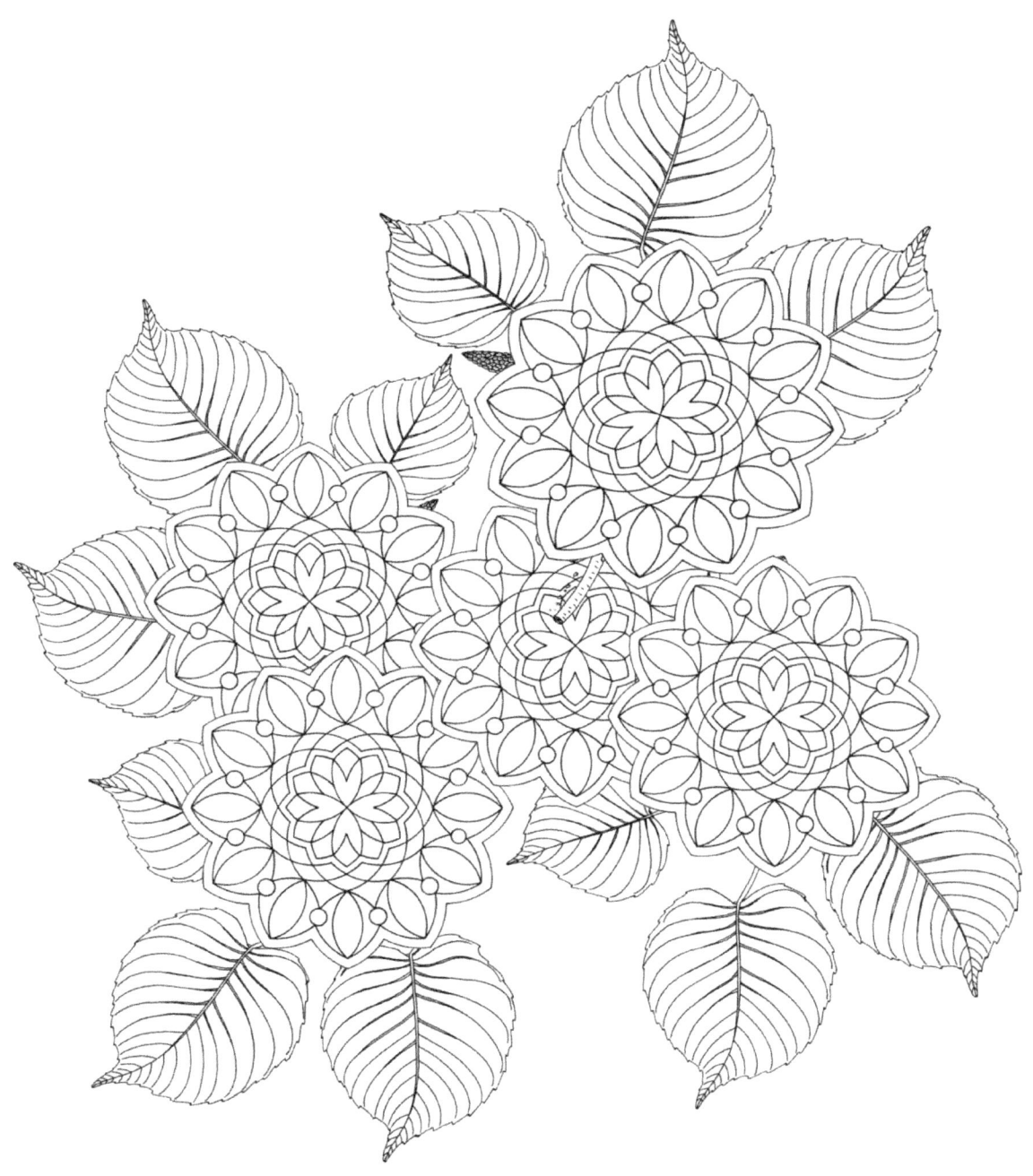

www.ingramcontent.com/pod-product-compliance
Lightning Source LLC
Chambersburg PA
CBHW080633190526
45169CB00009B/3383